THANK YOU

THANK YOU

101 WAYS TO PRACTICE
EFFORTLESS GRATITUDE

hatherleigh

))) hatherleigh

Thank You

Text copyright © 2012 Hatherleigh Press

Hatherleigh Press is committed to preserving and protecting the natural
resources of the Earth. Environmentally responsible and sustainable
practices are embraced within the company's mission statement.

Hatherleigh Press is a member of the Publishers Earth Alliance,
committed to preserving and protecting the natural resources of the
planet while developing a sustainable business model for the book
publishing industry.

This book was edited in the village of Hobart, New York. Hobart is a
community that has embraced books and publishing as a component of
its livelihood. There are several unique bookstores in the village. For
more information, please visit www.hobartbookvillage.com.

www.hatherleighpress.com

Library of Congress Cataloging-in-Publication Data is available
upon request.
ISBN: 978-1-57826-435-3

All Hatherleigh Press titles are available for bulk purchase, special
promotions, and premiums. For information about reselling and special
purchase opportunities, please call 1-800-528-2550 and ask for the
Special Sales Manager.

Cover Design by DCDESIGN
Interior Design by DCDESIGN

10 9 8 7 6 5 4 3 2 1

Printed in the United States

CONTENTS

Gratitude: *noun*

Etymology: Middle English, from Anglo-French or Medieval Latin; Anglo-French, from Medieval Latin *gratitudo*, from Latin *gratus* grateful

Date: 1523

: the state of being grateful : thankfulness

—MERRIAM-WEBSTER'S ONLINE DICTIONARY

A NOTE FROM THE PUBLISHER

This book began as a conversation with a friend many years ago. We had been discussing the importance of expressing gratitude even if the moment seemed to have already passed.

There is no time limit on a thank you. Whether a kindness or a courtesy goes unacknowledged for a day or a decade, there is no reason not to give thanks. Sometimes it's hard. Maybe we are embarrassed because we forgot so say thank you and then we feel it's too late. Well, it's never too late to show your gratitude.

There are many people who contribute to our lives directly and indirectly, in small ways and in very large ways. Parents, friends, teachers, employers, co-workers, ministers, neighbors, strangers— the list goes on. I can look back at many people in my own life who have given me much to be thankful for and to whom I owe a debt of gratitude. Hopefully I have reached them all in some way to show my appreciation. If not, I do express my thanks for the many ways they have made a meaningful difference in my life.

Showing gratitude can be a simple small gesture to a stranger who opens a door, holds a train, helps change a flat tire, lends their phone, or shares a smile. Gratitude and thankful gestures can be small ripples that, when added together, become a tidal wave of good will.

In this book, you will find 101 ways to practice effortless gratitude. Why effortless? Because showing gratitude should come easily. If it doesn't come easily to you now, then hopefully it will become more natural as you apply these thoughtful ideas to those people who come into your world.

Giving thanks also goes out to life's blessings. It is wise to recognize what we have rather than to remark as to what we don't. Take a moment to be grateful for the immensity of life itself.

Once learned and applied, gratitude and its companion, generosity, can together make for a better place for us all to live, work and exist. The human condition is fragile, but together we can form strong bonds of love and respect for each other, which can see us through difficult times that invariably come along and remind us to celebrate the good times that will come again.

So if it hasn't been said yet, say it now; "thank you".

With gratitude,

—ANDREW FLACH, PUBLISHER

PART I:
GRATITUDE AT HOME

Sometimes we forget to acknowledge those who know us best. No matter how frequently we may see or hear from family members, we can become so overwhelmed with small tasks that we miss our chances to express gratitude. Words of thanks are easy to share at any time of day, and they take only a few moments. For each person who is dear to us, reminding him or her of how thankful we are to have them in our lives will nurture loving relationships for years to come.

1

For one week, take a few minutes at the end of the day to thank each family member for something they do that contributes to everyone's well being. Recognizing the actions of others will help everyone end the day on a positive note and feel good about the day to come.

2

Offer to prepare a meal. The meal doesn't have to be elaborate—what is most important is that you make the effort to show your gratitude.

3

Leave a small gift where a family member can find it with a note that says, "Thank you!"

4

Take the time to express gratitude for a relative who passed away by gathering as a family to remember him or her. Take turns describing ways you are thankful for having had that person in your lives.

5 FREE WAYS TO SHARE GRATITUDE

1. WRITE A THANK YOU LETTER.
2. DO THE DISHES.
3. GIVE YOUR ATTENTION.
4. SHARE YOUR TIME.
5. GO FOR A WALK TOGETHER.

5

Prepare a cup of coffee or tea for your spouse or family member in the morning and take a few moments to thank them for all they do.

6

On Mother's Day, Father's Day, and Grandparent's Day, encourage your children to list 5 things about their parent or grandparent they are thankful for. Do the same for your own parent or grandparent.

7

Perform someone else's chores
without being asked. Your
actions will express your
appreciation.

8

Carefully listen to each other during the family meal. Allowing someone to share their thoughts shows your gratitude and appreciation.

9

Make a list of up to 10 reasons
why you are thankful to have
a family member in your life,
and either leave it in a place for
them to find, or personally share
it with them when you have a
moment together.

"When a person doesn't have gratitude, something is missing in his or her humanity. A person can almost be defined by his or her attitude toward gratitude."

—Elie Wiesel,
AUTHOR AND TEACHER

10

Sometimes getting out of the house can mean a lot. Take a family member out for a cup of coffee, a snack, or a walk through the park.

11

Don't wait until Thanksgiving
to be thankful. At least once
a week, take a few moments
before each meal for everyone at
the table to express their grati-
tude for each other.

12

Send a letter to a relative. Your correspondence will express your gratitude for the role this person has played in your family history.

"Gratitude is the fairest blossom which springs from the soul."

—HENRY WARD BEECHER,
CONGREGATIONALIST CLERGYMAN,
SOCIAL REFORMER AND ABOLITIONIST

13

Be thankful for the support of
your parents. Send a brief note
to your mother or father thank-
ing them for influencing your
life and inspiring you to follow a
dream or goal.

14

Surprise your loved ones by cleaning one area of the home and leaving them a simple note that says, "thank you for all you do."

15

Be sure to give a sincere and
heartfelt thank you to a child
when they perform a task, no
matter how small. You will pro-
vide encouragement and help
to nurture a spirit of generosity
within them.

16

Show gratitude for the gift of a new life when a baby joins the family by making a donation to an orphanage or children's hospital. True family is not limited to those we know, but extends to all people in need.

17

Plan a special night to throw a party as a family, and ask each "guest" to bring a small gift for someone. Then, share the gifts along with thoughts about your thankfulness for each other.

18

A heartfelt letter can mean so much more than a gift. Around the holidays, encourage your child to come up with five ways they feel thankful for a favorite teacher. Then, share those thoughts with the teacher in a letter.

19

Express your thanks for your family's blessings by giving back to others. Contribute to the community by volunteering together.

20

Gratitude can bring peace. If members of the family are fighting, ask them to set aside their argument and instead focus on what they appreciate about each other.

21

Family lifts us up when we are feeling down. Once difficult times have passed, be sure to express your thanks for your family's support by saying, "Thank you for being there."

PART II:
GRATITUDE WITH FRIENDS

It is easy to think that those closest to us know all our thoughts and feelings. This may mean we assume our friends know how thankful we are for them. However, sharing gratitude with someone else is important no matter how well we know each other. Giving thanks can be simple, and the benefits powerful. Any time we take to show how grateful we are for a friend enriches our lives and strengthens our bonds.

"Appreciation can make a day, even change a life. Your willingness to put it into words is all that is necessary."

—MARGARET COUSINS,
WRITER AND EDITOR

22

Send a thank you note to a friend
to express your sincere gratitude
for something they have done
for you . . . or just thank them for
being who they are.

23

Thank a friend for something they've done by giving them a warm hug the next time you see them.

24

Show that you appreciate a
friend by offering to set aside
your time to join them in
whatever activity they would
like . . . the choice is theirs!

"I awoke this morning with devout thanksgiving for my friends, the old and the new."

—RALPH WALDO EMERSON,
PHILOSOPHER, LECTURER,
ESSAYIST AND POET

25

The next time you enjoy a gift
from a friend, let them know.
Your communication will convey
a special "thank you."

26

When a friend does you a favor, be sure to send a thank you note that expresses your appreciation. Don't worry if you are at a loss for words; taking the time to write and mail a note communicates your gratitude in a heartfelt way, even if the letter is not long.

27

Sometimes we make the mistake of taking someone for granted. Take a few minutes to write down your thoughts on why you are thankful to have a certain friend in your life. Then, the next time you see them, be sure to let them know how much they mean to you, and why.

5 WAYS TO SAY THANK YOU THAT TAKE NO TIME

1. SHARE A SMILE.
2. OFFER A HUG.
3. SAY "THANK YOU SO MUCH" WITH SINCERITY.
4. SEND A QUICK E-MAIL.
5. LEAVE SOMEONE A SHORT NOTE.

28

Express your gratitude for having a friend in your life by giving them a call to find out how they are. When they speak, focus on listening to what they have to say and giving them your full attention.

"Let's be grateful for those who give us happiness; they are the charming gardeners who make our soul bloom."

—MARCEL PROUST,
FRENCH NOVELIST, ESSAYIST AND CRITIC

29

Revisit a memory of a special
time you spent with a friend.
Share photos or other souvenirs
and thank them for spending
that time with you.

30

Share your appreciation for a friend with someone else you know. Introduce two of your friends with a common interest to encourage their hobbies.

31

Spending time with a friend on their birthday is a great way to show you care. If you are unable to attend a celebration, be sure to set aside time to meet up with them, or send a special card or gift.

32

The best way to show your thanks for having someone in your life is to offer acceptance and encouragement. If one of your friends is feeling negative, help them to feel better by reminding them of their unique strengths.

33

When saying thank you to a friend for attending a special event, be sure to be specific. You can mention why it is you so valued their company by mentioning what they contributed to the party, such as lively conversation, or help with setting up. Or just thank them for being themselves and sharing their time with you and your guests.

34

Say "thank you" to a friend in a creative way. Choose one of their favorite things and incorporate it into a gift or a note card to personalize your expression of gratitude and make it unique.

35

Life can get hectic, but it only takes a moment to share your appreciation for someone. Send a brief e-mail to a friend letting them know you are thinking of them and hope to speak with them soon.

36

When invited to an event or social gathering, express your thanks for being included by offering to help the host or hostess.

37

We are influenced by others in so many ways. The next time you think of a friend's recommendation, prepare a meal from a recipe they gave you, or follow their advice, give them a call or send an e-mail to thank them for enriching your life.

38

Giving someone your undivided attention is a powerful way to express appreciation without words. When you are meeting with a friend, turn off your phone and any other electronic device, so you can completely focus on your companion.

39

Express your thanks for having
a friend in your life by letting go
of old grudges. Freeing yourself
from the past will enrich the
future for the both of you.

40

If you have to reschedule an
event with a friend, be sure to
take a moment to thank them
for their understanding.

41

Surprises can lift the spirits.
The next time you meet a friend,
surprise them with a small gift.

PART III:
GRATITUDE AT WORK

During the work week, we spend most of our time with colleagues. Yet we can be so focused on the work at hand that we forget how important it is to acknowledge one another's contributions. It only takes a few moments to make someone feel good about what they do—and this can make all the difference. Showing that you appreciate someone's efforts not only makes the day more pleasant, but it also fosters a positive working atmosphere. A feeling of camaraderie provides motivation, improves productivity, and reminds everyone that true success is defined by being considerate towards one another.

42

We often forget to thank those
who we don't see every day.
When communicating with col-
leagues in another office, take
the time to express your thanks
with a sincere e-mail, or give
him or her a call to express your
thanks.

43

After completion of a big project,
share your appreciation for your
employees' efforts by treating
them to lunch or coffee. Be sure
to start off the get-together
with sincere words of thanks.

44

At the end of the year, make the effort to thank every person in your department either in person, through an e-mail, or with a brief phone call.

45

A meaningful gift doesn't have to be a physical object. If someone shares knowledge or expertise with you, be sure to thank them promptly with a kind e-mail or a note.

"The essence of all beautiful art, all great art, is gratitude."

—FRIEDRICH NIETZSCHE,
GERMAN PHILOSOPHER

46

Take the time to ask someone how they are doing. Your concern for their well-being will express your gratitude for their role as a team member.

47

Even if you can't respond to a
request right away, acknowledge
receipt of an individual's e-mail
and let them know you will
take care of the task as soon as
possible.

Don't forget to thank those peo-
ple "behind the scenes." Learn
the names of those who work
in office services and be sure to
personally thank them for their
efforts.

49

If someone comes through for you by helping out with a last-minute task, show your appreciation by offering to assist them with whatever you can.

50

Share your appreciation for your employees by taking the time to listen to their concerns or suggestions. A brief meeting every once in a while to hear what they have to say is all it takes.

"Gratitude makes sense of our past, brings peace for today, and creates a vision for tomorrow"

—MELODY BEATTIE, AUTHOR

51

If someone takes the time to meet with you or goes above and beyond to fill a request, acknowledge their efforts with a handwritten thank you note. The note can be a brief expression of gratitude, and it will be appreciated long after it is opened.

52

Respecting other's time is an impactful way to show gratitude. When someone reaches out to you with a query, respond to them promptly and thank them for following up with you.

53

If you experience conflict in
the workplace, be the first to
apologize or initiate a resolu-
tion between two other people.
Thank them for getting over
past mistakes and moving
forward together towards
improvement.

54

Show your appreciation for your co-workers by keeping communal areas neat. Leave a note thanking the next person for doing the same.

55

During meetings, listen carefully to others before speaking. Being attentive shows your gratitude for someone else's ideas and encourages teamwork.

"Gratitude is not only the greatest of virtues, but the parent of all the others."

—CICERO, ROMAN PHILOSOPHER

56

Be sure to add a "thank you" to your work-related requests, and follow up by thanking the individual once the task is done.

57

Enjoy some time outside of the office with an employee or co-worker and share with them reasons why you are thankful for their contribution.

58

After someone thanks you for something you've done, show your appreciation for their acknowledgment with a sincere, "You're welcome."

59

If a co-worker has had a rough day, leave a small note on their desk for them to find the next day. Your gesture will show that you appreciate their ability to take on challenges.

If you thank someone in an
e-mail, follow up by walking
over to thank them in person.
Addressing someone face-to-face
sends a strong message of your
true appreciation.

61

On Thanksgiving, leave a message on your employees' voicemails expressing your thanks for their hard work and making them aware that you appreciate their contribution. This heartfelt message will last long after the holiday has come and gone.

62

Whether or not you end up taking someone up on their offer to help with a task, be sure to thank them sincerely for making themselves available.

63

If you have to reschedule a
meeting, be sure to thank your
co-workers for finding another
available time for you.

PART IV:
GRATITUDE IN THE WORLD

In the course of a single day, we see faces we've never seen before and exchange words with people we've never met. By the end of the day, these individuals are often forgotten. But brief interactions with strangers are opportunities. Each moment we spend with someone new—whether it's chatting for a few minutes or sharing a friendly smile—presents us with the chance to share gratitude and spread good will. Even if we never learn someone's name, being kind and expressing our thanks serves to remind us that all relationships have the power to enrich our lives.

64

Always look someone in the eye
when you say, "thank you."

65

For one day, make the effort to
smile at every person you meet.
A simple smile is a powerful way
to say "thank you" to others for
sharing your day.

66

In the course of your travels, even if you only interact with someone briefly, take a moment to express a genuine "thank you" for their help. Often it is the guidance of people we have just met that helps us get to where we are going.

When shopping at a store, ask the name of the person who is helping you. Then, thank them by name. This will make your "thank you" all the more meaningful.

"At times our own light goes out and is rekindled by a spark from another person. Each of us has cause to think with deep gratitude of those who have lighted the flame within us."

—ALBERT SCHWEITZER,
GERMAN THEOLOGIAN AND PHILOSOPHER

68

There are many people who make our lives easier who we rarely think to thank. The next time you see your postman or deliveryman, take a moment to find out their name and thank them sincerely for all their hard work.

69

If you witness someone helping someone else, let that person know you saw their act of generosity and tell them that you are thankful for the kindness they are bringing into the world.

70

Express your gratitude for the companionship and support of your fellow man by respecting everyone with whom you interact—even if the circumstances are stressful, remember to be kind.

"Kindness is the language which the deaf can hear and the blind can see."

—MARK TWAIN, AUTHOR

71

If you are lost and someone pro-
vides you with detailed direc-
tions, be sure to look them in
the eye and let them know how
much you appreciate their time
and attention.

72

After an enjoyable meal in a restaurant, express your gratitude to your server by providing a tip and, on your way out, make a point to thank the hostess or manager and let them know your server did a great job.

73

If you receive an invitation to an event, express your appreciation for being invited by replying promptly.

"Appreciation is a wonderful thing. It makes what is excellent in others belong to us as well."

—Voltaire,
AUTHOR, PHILOSOPHER

74

Remember that your closest
friends were once strangers.
Honor the gift of friendship and
express your thanks by being
friendly to those you encoun-
ter, even those whom you have
never met.

75

Enrich your "thank you" to someone who helps you by complimenting them on their performance. They will feel appreciated and proud.

76

After you read an article or a book that you find inspiring, send a note to the author to thank him or her. Your words will be appreciated.

77

If you ask someone for guidance or help and they are unable to assist you, be sure to take a moment to sincerely thank them anyway for their time and effort.

78

No matter how brief your
encounter may be with another
person, be sure to look them in
the eye to show you appreciate
their attention.

79

Always be courteous on the phone,
even with someone you've never
met. Be sure to let them finish
talking before you speak, and
thank them for their time even if
the call is brief.

PART V:
GRATITUDE FOR LIFE

Sometimes we become so preoccupied with our problems, goals, or daily "to do" list that we forget to be thankful for the blessings that are right in front of us. Every day, we should take a few moments to give thanks for what we have. This spirit of gratitude will provide energy and open our eyes to all the good things around us. Each one of us is blessed in so many ways, and acknowledging those blessings is the key to tapping into the power and wonder of life.

80

If you don't have the time or opportunity to thank someone, take a moment to think "thank you" and recall what you are thankful for. A spirit of gratitude enriches the world.

81

Every morning, take a few
moments to feel gratitude for
the gift of life.

"He is a wise man who does not grieve for the things which he has not, but rejoices for those which he has."

—EPICTETUS,
GREEK PHILOSOPHER

82

At the end of each day, make
a list of your blessings. These
can range from larger bless-
ings, such as the gift of friends
or family, to smaller blessings,
such as something beautiful you
noticed during the day or a meal
that you enjoyed.

83

After attending a cultural event or institution, express your gratitude by sharing your experience with others and encouraging them to go as well.

84

Share your gratitude for your daily meals by giving to others. Volunteer at a local soup kitchen or make a donation to an organization that feeds those in need.

5 WAYS TO BE THANKFUL FOR THE EARTH'S GIFTS

1. BE THANKFUL FOR THE AIR. TAKE A DEEP BREATH AND EXPRESS YOUR GRATITUDE.
2. BE THANKFUL FOR THE EARTH. AT LEAST ONCE A WEEK, TAKE A LONG WALK OUTDOORS.
3. BE THANKFUL FOR THE WATER. BE CONSCIENTIOUS ABOUT HOW MUCH WATER YOU USE AND APPRECIATE THIS LIMITED RESOURCE.
4. BE THANKFUL FOR THE EARTH'S BOUNTY. TAKE A MOMENT TO APPRECIATE YOUR FRESH FRUITS AND VEGETABLES AND CONSIDER HOW MUCH TIME AND CARE WENT INTO THEIR GROWTH.
5. BE THANKFUL FOR THE CYCLE OF THE SEASONS. IT IS THE PROCESS OF CHANGE THAT MAKES GROWTH POSSIBLE.

85

Express your thanks for the earth's natural beauty by making an effort to reduce waste. For one week, avoid using plastic bottles or cutlery and cut down on paper napkins. Then, turn those actions into habits so they become routine.

86

Share your gratitude for life's gifts with others. The next time someone gives you a present, donate an item of equal value to a local charity, or give a gift in their name.

87

If you regularly enjoy a local park or other recreational area, make it a point to set aside some funds to sponsor the upkeep of that location. Expressing your thanks in this manner is an active way to contribute to your community.

88

Show your gratitude for life by
living in the present moment.

89

Instead of focusing on what you don't have, practice feeling grateful for something that you hope to attain. This will give you the inner direction and motivation you need to achieve your goal.

*"Feeling grateful or apprecia-
tive of someone or something in
your life actually attracts
more of the things that you
appreciate and value into your
life."*

—CHRISTINE NORTHRUP, M.D.,
AUTHOR, DOCTOR, AND A LEADING
PROPONENT OF HEALTHFUL LIVING

90

Plant a flower or a tree in honor of someone you love. This meaningful "thank you" gift will be enjoyed by generations to come.

91

Share thanks with the men and women who serve our country. Set aside some time with friends and family to write thank you notes to troops serving overseas.

92

When you experience stress,
take a deep breath and allow
yourself to feel thankful for your
health. A feeling of gratitude
will help you get through life's
challenges.

"If the only prayer you ever say in your entire life is thank you, it will be enough."

—MEISTER ECKHART,
GERMAN THEOLOGIAN,
PHILOSOPHER AND MYSTIC

93

Be thankful for the earth's bless-
ings. Take a few seconds each
day to look up to the sky and
feel gratitude (no matter what
the weather may be).

94

Pets bring great joy into our lives. In addition to giving your pet treats or toys, show your appreciation by making a donation to a local shelter to aid animals that are less fortunate.

95

Our health is a great gift. Show your appreciation for your own strength by offering help, hope, or just good company to someone who is ill.

"*As we express our gratitude, we must never forget that the highest appreciation is not to utter words, but to live by them.*"

—John Fitzgerald Kennedy,
35th President of the United States

96

Take a moment to thank those
who have taught you life lessons
by sharing those lessons with
someone else.

97

The next time you go on a trip
and enjoy the natural beauty
of the area where you stayed,
show your appreciation by mak-
ing a donation to an organization
invested in protecting that land-
scape. Future generations will
experience the opportunity to
enjoy nature's gifts just as you
have seen them.

98

Express your thanks for the
benefit of your education
by donating to your school
or a reading center in your
neighborhood.

99

Just because you may have lost track of a friend doesn't mean that you can't take time to feel thankful that you knew them. Write a letter or list the ways that you appreciated that person and thank them for having been in your life.

Do not hang on to past hurts or regrets. Show your gratitude for the gift of the present by letting go of the past, and you will enjoy a fulfilling future.

Remember to take the time to thank yourself for all the work you do. Make a list of things you have accomplished in the last month of which you are proud.

"Thanks for being my friend
Thanks for thinking about me
Thanks for caring about me
Thanks for everything you did
for me
You shouldn't have
But I'm so glad you did."

—AUTHOR UNKNOWN

WHAT I AM GRATEFUL FOR

PEOPLE I AM GRATEFUL TO

MY IDEAS FOR SHOWING GRATITUDE

MY IDEAS FOR SHOWING GRATITUDE

MY IDEAS FOR SHOWING GRATITUDE

MY IDEAS FOR SHOWING GRATITUDE

MY IDEAS FOR SHOWING GRATITUDE